The Secrets of Powerful Advertising

Why More Customers Don't Respond to Advertising And How You Can Change That Today!

The Greater Business Institute

Franklin House Communications
Nashville

Copyright © 1998 by Michael S. Miller

All rights reserved. No part of this work may be reproduced, copied, stored in a retrieval system or transmitted in any form or by any means, graphic, electronic, mechanical, photocopying, recording, taping, or otherwise, without prior written permission of the publisher except in the case of brief quotation embodied in critical articles and reviews. For more information, address Franklin House Communications, P.O. Box 680035, Franklin, TN 37068.

Publishers Cataloging-in-Publication Data
The Greater Business Institute

    The 8 secrets of powerful advertising : why more customers don't respond to advertising and how you can change that today / by The Greater Business Institute

        p. cm.
    Includes bibliographical references and index.
    ISBN 0-9662692-6-8 (pbk.)
    1. Advertising. 2. Marketing I. The Greater Business Institute
    II. Title

                           98-070228

Illustrations by Tom Carter
Printed in the United States of America

10 9 8 7 6 5 4 3 2 1

CONTENTS

PREFACE

"Half the money I spend on advertising is wasted, and the trouble is I don't know which half."
David Ogilvy -
Confessions of an Advertising Man[1]

Ever wake up, all excited about the day, because that day you got to buy advertising? Chances are, you can query 10 business operators and not find one who enjoys buying advertising. Although some get a kick out of creating advertisements and some enjoy seeing or hearing their ads, few are overjoyed with the actual process of buying the stuff.

And no wonder. Advertising feels like gambling. It's a terrible feeling to pour a lot of money into advertising and never really know what impact it has had and what impact it will have in the future. (And without any warranties or 30-day money back guarantees on your advertising purchases, your comfort zone really can get stretched). To confound matters more, the business next door said that television works. Another colleague said it doesn't. An ex-boss was sold on newspapers. But the marketing guy would never touch them. What really does work?

Keep reading. Since "buying advertising" is not what you got into your line of work for, this book was designed to alert you to the guiding principles behind successful advertising. Just as there are fundamental principles behind driving a car, shooting a basketball or handling electrical wires, so too are there fundamental elements behind successful advertising.

Advertising used to be all guesswork. The current advertising person used to work for the previous advertising person who worked for the one before that. They all got their jobs because they did things the previous person's way. But no one knew if the job was being done correctly. How could they? All they knew was what the previous person told them. No one ever could determine if the previous person's advertising methods were right. They were guessing. Unfortunately, some businesses still operate this way. Change comes only when the individuals involved stop shying away from advertising study, and instead, embrace it.

This book won't be an exhaustive review of everything you could ever hope to know about advertising. Instead, it boils down volumes about the science of advertising to a few practical, fundamental elements which can validate (or invalidate) the advertising that you're doing today.

By just opening these pages, you're already getting a leg up on the competition. The good news is that most of your competitors have virtually no advertising training. They're playing the guesswork game. Learn the rules, and you'll be light years ahead of your competitors. You'll regularly be drawing new customers, and competitors will be wondering how. You'll have enough insight to make profitable and comfortable advertising investments. And when that consistently happens, buying advertising might not feel so bad after all.

When the word "advertising" is mentioned, the tendency is to think about writing and designing great ads, making sure the ads are the right color or size, and that they're running on the right days. That actually is only a part of what makes an advertising campaign profitable. Have the best looking or sounding ad in the world, but have your fundamental strategy out of line, and your advertising will accomplish little, if anything. As such, the focus here will be on advertising campaign fundamentals. In the following pages you'll find:

- The eight power principles that will make or break any advertising campaign.
- The degree to which each advertising vehicle allows you to incorporate advertising's fundamental power elements.
- The secrets of creating demand for your product or service.
- The keys to becoming a brand name or household word.

Right up front, some comforting news is that all advertising vehicles work - when used for the purposes they were designed for. Take a look at the text in the following print ad.

We Don't Need Any More Business!

Long's Sporting Goods has all the business it can handle. Please shop elsewhere!

The ad is ludicrous, right? If you were the fictitious Long's Sporting Goods, could you think of *any* advertising venue where you comfortably would place this message? Of course not. Why?

The ad might work! People might quit coming! The point is, all advertising vehicles can work. The trick is knowing how to effectively use each and then coming up with the plan that works for you.

"Plan" is an important word, because without it, it's way too easy to bounce from newspapers to cable TV to bus benches and back to papers, never seeming to come up with something that works consistently. Understanding advertising's foundational principles will keep you from buying advertising on impulse, and help you develop a cohesive, effective advertising strategy. Let the fun begin.

Research has come up with the best way to choose our advertising.

chapter 1

THE DANGERS OF CREATIVITY

Black and white. Right and wrong. In a world where few have the time or opportunity to learn the science of advertising, such absolutes all too often are forgotten. It simply is natural to hand off advertising to anyone with any experience putting together fun promotions. The rallying cry is often, "Forget all the rules. Put together the cutest or wildest promotions you can!" But frequently those entertaining ads and promotions overlook advertising's fundamental elements. These promotions break all the rules. And when they do, a lot of money can be wasted, and you may never even know it.

The first step in developing effective plans is to simply understand that <u>there are essential, foundational advertising principles</u> which, when violated, will render advertising and promotional programs ineffective. It's easy to let the real purpose of advertising get lost in the creativity. The granddaddy of advertising, David Ogilvy, warned that too many in the advertising community "worship at the altar of creativity - which means originality - the most dangerous word in the lexicon of advertising."[1]

As an example, recall the popular 1996 Nissan television commercial. Nissan's ad, featuring Barbie[2] doll and G.I. Joe doll look-a-likes was named by a host of major news publications as 1996's best commercial.[3] Yet that year Nissan's sales dropped sharply behind its competitors.

Nissan's sales were down three percent. The auto industry as a whole was *up* three percent while Nissan's primary competitors, Honda and Toyota, were both up at least twice that.[4] Nissan's ads were creative, but creativity in and of itself, is not enough to achieve advertising's basic goal. That goal is to have consumers say, "That's a great product. I want it now," not "That's a great looking, entertaining ad."

Any ad campaign can win industry awards for creativity yet still not sell product. Favor "fun," "wild" and "creative" over the science of advertising and pretty soon you'll utter that famous phrase, "My advertising isn't working!"

As such, common starting points like "How to write an effective ad" and "Which advertising vehicles should my ad run in?" initially will be set aside. Instead, the eight principles of powerful advertising first will be outlined. Violate any one of them and your advertising campaign could become useless.

chapter 2

MAKING YOURSELF KNOWN

You can advertise until you're entirely out of money, and still not adequately create an awareness of your business or unique selling proposition. You could advertise on the biggest station or paper in town, and still end up in the same position. That's because all advertising is worthless if it's not properly presented to its intended recipients. Let's focus on how to become known - how to become a household word.

Successful advertising capitalizes on "reach" and "frequency." Ever been quoted circulation figures by the local newspaper or audience sizes by a radio or television station? Those figures are "reach." Reach is the number of different people that listen to a station each week or read a single edition of a paper or magazine. (It is not necessarily the same as the number of people who actually will *see* or *hear* your message). Frequency is how many times people actually see or hear your ad.

Most advertising vehicles don't reach lots of people *and* reach them frequently, so it's important to know how reach and frequency are interrelated. To answer, think about why your customers do business with you. When you really get down to it, they do business with you because they trust you and your products. And why do they trust you? At some point in time, you've gained credibility with them. They're comfortable with you. Without that single ingredient, your customers would be shopping elsewhere.

How do you get comfortable with something? Through frequent contact, exposure or experience with it. The people who do business with you do so because through some sort of frequency mechanism, they've become comfortable with you. That comfort leads to confidence and trust in you which in turn leads to sales.

Frequency: Again and Again and Over and Over

To optimize any sort of frequent, comfort-building, confidence-raising, credibility-enhancing contact with your prospect, an individual consumer should see or hear your ad at least three times.[1] Anything less than that, and there's no real understanding of your message. Your advertising will have little impact other than to take money out of your wallet. Three is the critical number and that doesn't mean reaching your prospects once at the beginning of the year, once in the summer and once the following winter. The frequency has to happen in a short time period.

Frequency works just like you worked when you were learning how to read or how to multiply. You probably had flash cards that you reviewed over and over again. You didn't review the letter "A" sound or the letter "B" sound or what 3 times 4 is once in second grade, once in third grade and once in fourth grade. You went over that information constantly - every day - maybe even several times a day. It was hammered into your brain again and again. Similarly, your goal should be to hit as much of a medium's audience as possible three or more times in very short time periods.

The Hmmm Thing

Why three? Consider how the typical consumer might respond to your advertisement. A landmark 1972 study published in the Journal of Advertising Research showed that in her first contact with your ad the consumer simply asks, "What is it?"[2] Regardless of whether the advertised brand will be perceived as being good or bad, the first exposure is just an attention getting device. The consumer thinks, "Hmmm, what's this? I haven't heard this before." And then she likely blocks out any further thoughts of your message until she's hit with it again.

The second time she is exposed to your ad she may realize she's heard it before and wonder, "What of it?" She's determining whether the advertised product or service has any personal relevance.

The third exposure becomes a reminder. It reminds her to determine whether or not this advertisement has brought up any issues which must be fulfilled. This is where she can say, "This sounds good. I want this."

These responses all assume that the consumer has both an interest in the advertised product and is in the market for the product. When these assumptions aren't in place, more recent analysis suggests that you must reach an individual consumer 10 or more times just to communicate the product's brand name and existence, and that 12 to 15 exposures may be necessary to communicate new copy claims.[3]

Sounds like the old quotation about the impact of frequency:

"The first time a man looks at an
    advertisement, he does not see it.
The second time he does not notice it.
The third time he is conscious of its existence.
The fourth time he faintly remembers having
    seen it before.
The fifth time he reads it.

The sixth time he turns up his nose at it.

The seventh time he reads it through and says, "Oh brother!"

The eighth time he says, "Here's that confounded thing again."

The ninth time he wonders if it amounts to anything.

The tenth time he thinks he will ask his neighbor if he has tried it.

The eleventh time he wonders how the advertiser makes it pay.

The twelfth time he thinks perhaps it may be worth something.

The thirteenth time he thinks it must be a good thing.

The fourteenth time he remembers that he has wanted such a thing for a long time.

The fifteenth time he is tantalized because he cannot afford to buy it.

The sixteenth time he thinks he will buy it some day.

The seventeenth time he makes a memorandum of it.

The eighteenth time he swears at his poverty.

The nineteenth time he counts his money carefully.

The twentieth time he sees it, he buys the article, or instructs his wife to do so."[4]

In a best case, does all this mean that running an ad three times will do the trick? If only it were so simple. This consumer is not only doing the "Hmmm" thing with your ad, she's doing it to thousands of other ads as well. She faces a constant bombardment of advertisements. (Some estimates say that the average consumer faces 3000 marketing impressions every single day[5]). Since only one out of nine ads ever get through to the targeted customer, your message really has to fight for attention.[6]

And because your ad must be seen or heard three times before you can achieve the desired results, you in essence have to get your ad in front of targeted customers almost 30 times before it's seen or heard three times by any individual. Even putting forth 40-50 advertising impressions in a one week time period (and around 80 in two to three days to promote a sale) is not overkill. So many

> **The greater the number of advertising exposures, the higher the actual and planned usage of your product.[7]**

impressions are often necessary to break through all the clutter and to get your message out ahead of the 3000 other impressions seen or heard that day.

With any fewer ads, you're throwing money away. Too few prospects will have three exposures to your ad and therefore, won't have enough recollection of your business to bring you the business you deserve.

Is frequency sounding pretty important? Absolutely! But isn't this type of frequency overdoing it? Absolutely not. Even when an individual consumer is exposed to your message more than three times, it's not overkill. With each exposure, your advertising's effectiveness continues to grow. After three exposures, the effectiveness doesn't grow as rapidly as it once did, but it nevertheless grows.[8] Nor does this level of frequency wear out the effectiveness of ads and campaigns so long as the campaigns are delivering the appropriate message.[9]

With the relative significance of frequency, it is interesting to note that the much-ballyhooed importance of getting a single ad in front of the largest audience possible diminishes. In other words, frequency has nothing to do with the size of any individual medium's audience. And because of frequency's importance, circulation figures and audience ratings (i.e, "Reach") cannot be used as accurate gauges in and of themselves of the return you'll get on your money. Getting your message in front of prospects over and over and over again is much more important than the size of the advertising vehicle used to convey your message.

Dominate!

To succeed, you have to communicate frequently in short time spans. The quickest way to get your message out frequently is to become an important advertiser to the advertising vehicle that you do use. Your goal should be to find an advertising vehicle that you can dominate. This is war and you need to establish a beachhead. Taking a big percentage of your advertising budget and pouring it into a single medium lets you dominate that medium.

Becoming a dominant entity may involve rearranging how your advertising dollars are spent. For instance, instead of running seven ads a week in an advertising venue used by your primary customer group, you'll want to take all 28 ads for the month and run them in a single week. When you do this month after month you become larger than life to that venue's audience.

If all the money from a month or two of advertising isn't enough to buy appropriate frequency for even a one-week period, then your advertising vehicles are simply too big. They may be the right vehicles for others, but they're not right for you. Move to smaller advertising vehicles and buy appropriate frequency there. Instead of buying two ads on or in the largest station or paper in town, you may, for example, want to buy 50 in smaller entities that you can dominate. And if you can't dominate any given medium, then dominate a section of it, like late night broadcasting or the classifieds.

Establish your beachhead.

An added benefit to this fundamental principle is that it allows you to "flank" the competition. Lots of competitors are likely wasting money, fighting it out in advertising sections or entities that they really can't afford. By dominating a *different* arena, you can gain sizable consumer groups almost by default. Once you "own" an audience, your profits increase. So will your ad budget, meaning you can begin to branch out to dominate even more advertising entities. You'll be capturing the entire market one step at a time.

Let's summarize the relationship between reach and frequency this way:

> **"Although it costs about the same,**
> **reaching 5000 people 10 times each**
> **will always produce better results**
> **than reaching 50,000 people one time each".**

Reach is useless without frequency. Don't get hung up on the hoopla and sales hype attached to audience sizes, rates, cost per thousands, gross ratings points and the like. Instead, focus on where you can buy enough frequency to dominate a medium which reaches consumers likely to do business with you.

The Disappearing Act

Important question: "What if you can't afford to maintain this type of frequency week in and week out, or even every second or third week?" Answer: "Only advertise in the weeks when you can afford to get the necessary frequency." Won't your business fall apart during the weeks that you're not advertising? No! People will still remember you! Your ads will have been pounded into their brains. You'll be like McDonalds,[10] Coke and Tide who, on a national scale, do the same thing. You may not have been exposed to any of their commercials in the past two months, but you always feel like you came across one in the last few days. And when you stop to think about fast food or soft drinks or detergents, you always think of these companies or products first.

> **Frequency helps people retain your message.**

When messages have been pounded home, people subconsciously store them until they have use for them.[11] Frequent repetition pushes messages into people's brains so often that they still think they saw or heard these ads last week. Even though you likely won't use the national media that Coke and McDonalds do, any business, by scheduling ads in an appropriate manner in its own markets, can accomplish the same thing. And when this is done, all month long customers and revenues will continue to increase.

As an aside, it's amazing to see the same thing happen in the media outlets which run your ads. It's not unusual to hear the media employees say, "I'm sick and tired of that ad," when in fact, the ad they're referring to hasn't run in months. Frequency is very powerful.

So let's say you have a $15,000 annual advertising budget and a campaign that dominates any given vehicle costs $3000. What do you do? You only run your campaign five times a year. If you spread the ads out thinner, they'll just get swallowed up by the thousands of other ads out there each day.

By having an ad campaign running more than five weeks out of the year, you'd "reach" more total people than you would by running just five times a year. But you'd give up frequency. Even though you would be advertising across more weeks, you'd be hitting the average consumer, at best, only one time. Unless the consumer is already on her way out the door to buy your product category (and you'll always reach some people like that) that one advertising impression will be ineffective.[12]

When you concentrate your ads in short time periods, it's like firing tons of ammunition. You're hitting quickly and with power. You're sending a message that will stick with people. The key to becoming known is to rapidly deliver at least three advertising impressions (through many more advertisements) to your prospect base.

Advertising Power Secret #1: Concentrate on frequency, not reach.

chapter 3

HOW TO CREATE DEMAND

*Don't wait for prospects
to put themselves in the market
for your product or service.
Draw them into the market yourself!*

W e now know that most advertising options can be categorized as either a reach vehicle or a frequency vehicle. Similarly, advertising choices can also be tagged as those which **motivate** consumers to buy, or those which **inform** consumers about products and services. As we'll soon see, most buying decisions are actually emotional decisions, not informed ones. As a result, advertising media which capitalize on emotions, and motivate consumers to buy put much more money in your bank account than media which simply inform.

Understanding the Buying Process

The vast majority of all purchases are made for emotional reasons and justified logically. Let's say that you're thinking about buying a new car. You read the newspaper every day and you go through all of the auto dealer ads. You start getting the feeling that all the dealers are kind of alike. You know what payment range to expect. You know who has the widest selection. You know who currently has a rebate offer. Yet none of these are issues that will make you choose one dealer over another.

What you don't know is who is going to be comfortable to do business with. You don't know who is going to rip you off and who is not. You don't know who is going to treat you like you deserve to be treated and who is not. All of these unanswered issues are, in essence, emotional factors that will be at the core of your decision. Whoever provides security on these issues is going to have a very good chance of selling you an automobile.

Let's carry this beyond choosing a dealer and look at choosing a particular model. Noted marketing strategist Jack Trout cites the phenomenon of the four wheel drive sport utility vehicles.[1] Let's say you want to buy one of these. They have been, after all, huge sellers. In the ads for these vehicles, they're shown going over rough, wild terrain. Yet in real life, very few of them are actually taken off road.

Why do they sell? For emotional reasons - not logical ones. They make people feel good. Some people buy because their dreams of what they want to be like relate to the wild outdoors. Others buy because the guy moving up the ladder at work has one and so does that guy's boss. When you have one it means you're doing what's acceptable. You're not going out on a limb. You're adding to your sense of security.

The underlying point is that the purchase is made for an emotional reason. How is the purchase justified? "Oh, you can take it off road!" And perhaps it's further justified by saying, "Plus, when I stretch out the payments an extra year it's really affordable." *The decision to buy is made for an emotional reason. The decision then is justified by a logical reason.*

The logical justification doesn't have to make total sense.

But people always do find what they think will be a good, logical reason to justify the emotionally-based decision they just made.

> *People buy what they really want to buy,*
> *whether it's logical or not.*

Another case in point: One of our colleagues recently made a computer purchase. Almost immediately, he settled on a manufacturer, simply because he felt that vendor probably did more business with the type of people he felt he was like. Did the manufacturer sell the best product? That wasn't the point. Since the decision to use that manufacturer had already been made, the next step was to justify that decision. This didn't mean determining if that manufacturer sold the best product, but rather proving (justifying) that it did.

That took a couple more weeks as the buyer examined all the details and ratings pertaining to several brands and vendors, until he had enough information to say, "Yes, logically, this is a good product." He could now justify his buying decision. But the real decision was not based on any logic and had been made long before the logic was in place.

No matter what the product, all of your sales are made because they fulfill an emotional need. They reach something at the core of people. And that something virtually always starts with a need to have a comfort level with, and a confidence in the potential place of purchase. Without establishing that first, there is no sale.

Once that foundational comfort zone is achieved, additional emotional needs can be addressed. Some purchases are made simply because the product makes the buyer feel secure (i.e. "I didn't go out on a limb and do something everyone else might think is silly"). Some are made because the product fulfills a desired image or lifestyle.

H.A. Maslow's study of human motivation suggests that our first purchases are made to fulfill basic physiological requirements like water or food. We're then motivated by things which provide security, protection and stability. Next, we're motivated by love for those dear to us, followed by esteem (prestige, status, achievement), and lastly by self-actualization (maximizing one's potential).[2] Regardless of where one's at on the physiological needs ladder, the decision to buy is made through an emotion-based process.

On the flip side of the consumer whose emotional need has been met is a very different animal. Here we have the informed consumer. This person understands what product lines and brands you carry. She's seen your price and item advertising. She knows about your rebates, your wide selection and payment plans. She knows as much about you as any consumer does. But she's not coming in your store.

Either you haven't developed her confidence in you as a retailer, or you haven't hit a need that she's aware she has. There is no demand from her for your product. As a result, she simply doesn't care enough to get in her car, drive down the street and come in your door. You're not important to her (regardless of whether logic says you should be). No amount of information can convince her to want what it is you do or sell.

Ads which impact the emotional portion of the decision-making process have the power to create demand. They can motivate consumers before the decision to buy has been made. Conversely, informative ads are only good after the demand has been created and the consumer's decision to buy has been made. Once that happens, consumers then may seek out and pay attention to information you wish to convey. But the inherent logic found in informational ads will never, in and of themselves, create demand for your store.

Spend the bulk of your time and effort with consumers creating emotional demand by demonstrating "what's in it for them." Your advertising job is not to inform, but to

> **Don't spend a lot of time and money on ads which simply inform.**

persuade the average consumer to walk into your store. That comes when people have some sort of emotional reason to do business with you (maybe simply because they like you), not a logical one.

Because of the emotion-based decision-making process, does information become useless? Of course not. After all, this is the information age! Think back to our computer buyer. Once people are predisposed (e.g. motivated and persuaded) to purchase a product category or service, or attend an event (like a sale!) they need information to logically justify their decision.

Information ads allow people to sit down with the material and use the facts to justify their buying decision. Almost always, they've made the decision to buy; if not the specific brand, at least the product category. They just need information to validate their heartfelt desires. But those who are only informed, and not motivated, will never buy your product. If the bulk of your advertising isn't being used to persuade and motivate consumers, save your money.

Sound Advice

We've seen that the bulk of buying decisions are made for emotional reasons. We know that ads which impact the emotions have the power to influence people prior to the buying decision. Now we must determine which types of advertising venues best lend themselves to carrying all of this out. Let's begin by going outside of the advertising world and thinking back to Martin Luther King's "I have a dream" speech. The "I have a dream" line is a powerful line that most people have heard at one time or another. Compare the difference between reading that phrase on a printed page and actually hearing a tape of Martin Luther King saying it. It's like day and night. All of the feeling and *emotion* of that line are only captured when we *hear* it. People get charged up and ready for action only when they hear his words.

Do the same thing with man's first walk on the moon. Remember Neil Armstrong's words? "That's one small step for man; one giant leap for mankind." Again, there's a huge difference between reading his printed words and hearing him actually say them. People all across America fantasized about hopping around on the moon when they heard those words. But when they read those words, they usually skimmed over them as they made their way to the next paragraph.

Or think about a ball game. Eliminate the visual aspect by shutting your eyes at a sporting event or instead, listening to a game on the radio. The sound of the crowd cheering or the announcers screaming while a great play is made horribly overshadows a written description of it in the next day's paper. No amount of reading how the great football runner "danced by two defenders en route to a 72-yard touchdown run" can compare with the passion and *emotion* of *hearing* the real thing.

> # Our emotions and decision-making
> # are captivated by sound.

Not only are our emotions influenced by the presence of sound, they're also affected by the *way* things sound. Jack Trout cites two studies reflecting this. In one, two women, originally deemed to be of equal beauty, were assigned false names. The false name assigned to one was Jennifer and the false name assigned to the other was Gertrude. They were again judged on their beauty. No surprise here - Jennifer greatly out-gained Gertrude in the vote for the most beautiful, even though without names, they'd been judged to be of equal beauty. With the second vote, the women's looks hadn't changed. The only variable that changed was the sound associated with each woman.[3]

In a separate study, third grade teachers graded a set of children's compositions. Duplicate compositions from "David" and "Michael" were included, but the names on the duplicate set were changed to "Elmer" and "Hubert." Guess what? On the same compositions, David and Michael each got a "B" whereas Elmer and Hubert each got a "C."[4] Again, the way these children's names sounded had an enormous impact on the decision-making associated with test-grading.

Similarly, American Motors once tried to see what consumers would pay for a car it was introducing. It demonstrated the car to one group of consumers, but didn't put a name on the car. That group was willing to pay around $10,000 for the vehicle. Additional groups also were shown the car, with the car being identified by a different name to each group. Again, the sound of the name impacted what people would be willing to pay, with the group being told that the name would be "Renault Premier"[5] willing to pay $3000 extra![6]

Creating Demand

Emotional factors are at the root of most buying decisions. Advertisements impacting our emotional core can influence people prior to the buying decision. When we take advantage of the power that sound has on our emotional decision-making, we not only can influence people prior to their buying decisions, we can create demand for the product or service. This is, perhaps, the most important concept this book offers. The key aspect is that by using media containing sound, the prospect can be influenced before she ever even thinks of buying the product. There's no waiting until the prospect is in the market for whatever it is that you do or sell. You can draw her into the market now.

Let's say you're selling a supplementary reading product used by parents whose children are starting to fall behind in school. By using sound, you can create emotional settings which make the parents start to feel guilty. They feel guilt because they suddenly realize that they have the power to prevent any additional slide. They can keep that smiling little child that they've nurtured from day one from getting any further behind.

That guilt is at the core of the parents' beings. It motivates them to buy the product. *The advertisement, by driving home an emotional value, actually creates demand for the product.* It doesn't wait until someone makes the decision to seek help. The buyer is not already looking at similar products, trying to ascertain which one to buy. No! Getting supplemental help is nowhere on the buyer's mind until the ad comes along. The buyer is drawn into the market. Demand is created.

The only caveat is not to confuse creating demand with changing innate human behavior. The tools of advertising won't change the latter. No advertising in the world can make Florida residents take up snow skiing. On the other hand, increasing demand for fishing boats in Florida is a "do-able" task.

Long entrenched behavior is difficult to change. Getting people to adopt behaviors which compliment their emotional needs isn't. The power of sound helps here as it more easily creates the emotional settings which motivate and persuade people to make specific product purchases. It helps capitalize on emotions. It can drive purchases through the power of suggestion. It can create demand.

Consider the following broadcast ad which could be used by

a home security firm. (Yes, trying to convey the emotional impact of *sound* by *printing* the script is tricky).

(Sounds of someone breaking a window followed by burglars yelling out what they've found as they ransack a home):

Announcer (very serious tone talking over the noise):

> "You are listening to a burglary. One in ten homes in our town is burglarized every year. That means every 10 years there's a good chance your home will be burglarized. And there's no way you can *stop it*."

> (Noise ends as announcer says, "stop it." Two seconds of complete silence follow.)

> "Or is there? There is now a free booklet on ways you can protect your home from burglars - ways to make you feel safe when you're home alone. Call 1-800-xxx-yyyy for the free Home Security and Protection booklet. The number is 1-800-xxx-yyyy. Find out whether your home is easy prey for burglars. Get peace of mind about your home's safety for the next time you're away. Call 1-800-xxx-yyyy today, so this doesn't happen to you:"

> (Woman opens a door and screams, "Oh no!" Sirens flare up in the background.)

> "Call for your free Home Security and Protection booklet today. Call 1-800-xxx-yyyy. 800-xxx-yyyy."

By making the burglary real, the number of calls greatly increases. Callers learn that their home could be burglarized. More importantly, they're made to *feel* like it's going to happen, and possibly at any minute no less. They're suddenly drawn into the market for home security systems. It's the power of sound that allows you to influence consumers prior to the decision-to-buy and it's that power that draws new consumers into the marketplace.

Advertising Power Secret #2: Create demand. Use sound.

chapter 4 | BECOMING MEMORABLE

The third key to powerful advertising campaigns is to become memorable. Although being memorable might not translate directly into immediate sales, having a memorable identity helps you build top-of-mind awareness. It helps you build a brand name. You become the first business consumers think of when they're in the market for whatever it is you do or sell. Following up on our discussion of sound as a persuasive element, we find that sound also helps us remember things! People remember more if they hear words than if they see them.[1]

Let's run through a quick test. Can you fill in the blanks on these popular slogans of yesteryear?

(a) "Winston[2] tastes good like a _____."

(b) "Plop, plop, fizz, fizz, oh_____."

(c) "Two all beef patties, special sauce, lettuce, cheese, pickles, onions on a _____."

(d) "Roto-rooter, that's the name and away go_____."

The answers?	
a)	cigarette should
b)	what a relief it is (ad for Alka Seltzer)
c)	sesame seed bun (Big Mac)
d)	troubles down the drain

Although these slogans haven't aired for years, virtually everyone born before 1960 can instantly fill in the blanks. Did an entire generation memorize the Winston cigarette and Roto-rooter slogans on purpose? Of course not. Through the power of sound, these product identities were forcibly etched into the minds of entire generations. And the people who grew up with these slogans readily can identify these products today.

The real significance is that most of these ad slogans haven't been broadcast since the 1970s. In particular, the Winston slogan was banned from broadcast media in 1971, when the advertisement of cigarettes on TV and radio was made illegal.

In the years immediately following 1971, the makers of Winston spent countless advertising dollars in media other than TV and radio. It was all in a fruitless attempt to establish a new Winston identifier. Anyone remember, "Real People Want A Real Cigarette?" That was the focus of a 1987 campaign.[3] The cigarette was also positioned as "Real People. Real Taste. Winston - America's Best."[4] Yet nobody came to know those positions nor any other positions the company tried to develop. Why? They couldn't be heard.

The sounds associated with these products obviously made these products more than memorable. They became household words. They'd won the masses before the masses could ever look for competing ads in the phone books or newspapers.

Aren't old enough to remember any of those ads? How about these?

   (a) "American Express - Don't _____."

   (b) "That's what Campbell's soup is_____."

(c) "Kellogg's Frosted Flakes, they're _____."

(d) "Be - all that you can be - in_____."

(e) "Oh I wish I were an_____."

(f) "Pepsi, the taste of _____."

The answers:
a) "leave home without it."
b) "Mmm good."
c) "gr-r-r-r-eat!"
d) "the Army."
e) "Oscar Mayer wiener."
f) "a new generation" or
"generation next"

These brands all have top-of-mind awareness created through sound. Contrast those with the number of written ads you can recall from even yesterday's paper. "Sound" sticks in our minds and makes us remember things.

Just as most advertising choices either provide reach or frequency, and just as most media either provide persuasive or informative elements, advertising options can also be divided into "sound" and "no sound" categories. The use of sound is your key to becoming memorable.

Advertising Power Secret #3: Become memorable through sound.

He heard that love song on the elevator
and he can't get it out of his head.

chapter 5 | REACHING THE RIGHT PROSPECTS

We've learned how to use frequency, create demand and become memorable. The fourth key to powerful advertising is finding and speaking to the right prospect group. If you're a business owner, when you first got into business, you probably entered a field where you saw opportunity. You probably saw distinct sets of consumers who had specific wants and needs that you felt you could meet. Seeing such opportunities usually results in putting your focus on meeting the needs of one or more of these "target" consumer groups.

Distinct consumer segments are found in every industry. In the computer magazine industry "PC Novice[1]" targets those new to the personal computing world. "Home PC" is directed to the family which uses its PC primarily for pleasure. "PC Magazine" offers more of a technical orientation. Each publication has its own distinct consumer focus.

Whatever you sell, there are certain groups of people who are more prone than others to buy your product or service. They might be grouped based on easily defined attributes such as age, income and education, or they may be grouped by softer attributes such as interests, attitudes or aspirations.

Once in a while, a great product that many might buy is

promoted to the wrong consumer group. For instance, someone could promote retirement condominiums in a teenage magazine. The product is fine, and there are people who want it, but it is promoted to a target group which has no desire for it.

Fortunately, many advertising vehicles make it easy to target. Direct mail lets you contact only those who characteristically are similar to your customers. Radio stations deliver 24-hour a day fare intended for one type of customer group. If you need upper income, older adults, News/Talk stations deliver them. If young males are your primary customers, rock stations reach them while consumers with higher than average family and household purchases are reached by Christian stations. Magazines and some regional or community newspapers behave the same way, with each one reaching a different consumer group.

And when the whole entity doesn't focus on a sole consumer group, the parts of that entity sometimes do. For instance, various sections of the newspaper allow you to hone in on specific types of people. Readership of the sports section is predominantly male. The food section reaches a specific type of reader as does the entertainment section. TV programs provide similar breakouts. Daytime soaps usually are watched by females. Late night shows are watched by younger males.

Thus, a car dealer who sells different models, each for a distinct consumer set might use a specific TV show to talk with potential truck buyers. He might use another show for prospective station wagon owners, and a third for sports car buyers.

Finding the correct target group and customizing your message to fit it is a simple concept. Don't overlook it.

Advertising Power Secret #4: Target the right prospects.

chapter 6

NOT ALL PRODUCTS SELL

E ver try to advertise something that people just do not want? The slickest advertising campaign in the world will never create demand for chocolate covered ants, squid or spoiled milk. Similarly, the most brilliant advertising strategy known to man won't reverse the decline in railroad passenger travel or interest in the Ford Pinto[1]. Some products or offers simply have little appeal.

On the other hand, some products or offers gain instant attention. A jug of milk or a Mercedes Benz, advertised for one-fourth of their regular price, both would draw enormous crowds.

The products you advertise and the offers you promote are crucial pieces of your advertising campaign. They take on even greater significance when you're promoting a sale. Here are some rules of thumb concerning sale offers:

1)   Make a great offer. You want people to react quickly. The promoted sale items must be something most people require (like food) or items a lot of people would like to have (like the latest Disney video). If your goal is to move slow sellers, mark them down to a price they'll sell at, stack them next to the hot-selling items and then advertise only the hot-selling items. You'll sell more of the fast-movers and more of the slow-movers.

2)   Make your offer to the right target group.

3)   Advertise a price-point which allows people to purchase on impulse. That's usually under $20. Give buyers a reason to act quickly. Give a big discount - 35% or better, and say it as "Regularly $10, now just $5.99." Real dollars mean much more than percentages.

4)   Never say, "for a limited time only" or "while supplies last." Customers usually take such phrases to mean that they probably don't need to hurry in. Instead, enact deadlines. State that "the sale ends Sunday," or that "everyone who stops in by 9 o'clock Friday gets a free door prize."

Advertising Power Secret #5:   Promote appealing products with appealing offers.

On a nice day like today you'd think
all the shoppers would come by.

chapter 7

THE POWER OF WORDS

Remember from chapter 3 the important role emotions play in the buying process? It's critical to recognize that most of the strong emotions likely to move us to action - things like fear, guilt, pride or greed - are all just words and sounds. They're not pictures.

Neither are the concepts by which we're able to relate to most name brand products. When we hear someone say, "Miller Beer,[1]" what do we think of? Why, "it tastes great and is less filling." We think of a benefit derived from that beverage, not what the beverage looks like.

When we hear "Coke," we think of "the real thing," not of a glass containing a dark, fizzy liquid. What do we think of with Volvo? We think safety. What's Crest for? It's for fighting cavities. Nordstrom's department stores? They're service. All-State Insurance? They're the good hands people. State Farm? They're like a good neighbor. Burger King? It's flame-broiled taste. Wheaties? It's the breakfast of champions. Frosted Flakes? They're gr-r-r-eat. Little Caesar's Pizza? It's "pizza, pizza" - two pizzas for the price of one.

None of these concepts begin with a picture. Safety isn't a picture nor is service or flame broiled taste. Yet these are the attributes by which we recognize certain products. Each sales concept begins with an idea that's boiled down to a few simple words. *We remember the product by these words, not by visual images.*

On the other hand, what's the distinctive selling attribute of a Gateway computer? That's difficult to say. Although the company is a quality provider of mail order computers, its packaging and campaigns traditionally have not conveyed this. Instead, campaigns often have centered around visual images of black and white cows; images that are presumably links to the company's geographic location rather than its products' distinct selling points.

Yes, it's fun to have a cute visual. And it would be nice to tell everything there is to tell about you. No doubt that if it could, Little Caesar's would tell you they offer this kind of pizza and that kind of pizza and that the cheeses are a special kind and that the sausages are too, and on and on and on. But people mentally do not digest all that. They've got a million things going on in their minds. If you want to get through to them, you've got to boil down everything to a simple concept. That's all your prospects have time for and that means you'll have to sacrifice promotion of many of your product or service's other attributes.

Positioning

How do you know when you've boiled down everything to the "right" attribute? You begin by understanding the "positioning" concept.

The right position or attribute your product should own and be known for must be a simple one. It must fill a niche, or a hole. That niche must be something the human mind is willing to concede you. If competitor A is the established leader in the quality niche, and you come along and say that your quality is better, the customer's mind isn't going to believe you. It won't give you that position because the mind already has given that place to Competitor A. If you want a place in the prospect's mind, you've got to dislodge Competitor A or be something else. You can't communicate a position already held by someone else.

It often is helpful to determine what niche, if any, you already own. The prospect's perception is reality so whatever the prospect base already is willing to concede to you generally is the best place to start.

What types of niches generally are available? There are literally hundreds ranging from a high price (status) niche to a low price niche, from imported to American made, from safety to daring, from traditional to new, etc. Your chance for success lies in capturing a profitable niche identity not already owned by the market leader. (For more on this important concept, read the 1981 classic "Positioning" by Jack Trout and Al Ries, published by McGraw Hill).

Where Do The Pictures Go?

In determining your niche, it's important that you be able to concisely communicate it verbally. When we get hungry we don't draw a picture of a person holding an empty plate, then point at it and say, "This shows how I feel." We

> **The core of communication is words. It's not pictures. We retain more of the *message* when we *hear* the message.**

say, "I'm hungry!" *We say the words.* So too with advertising. In most circumstances, your message is communicated best when the core of your advertising campaign begins with a verbal concept, not a visual one.

When the heart of your campaign does focus on a visual (like a cow) instead of a core attribute (like safety), funny things happen. You're liable to produce very entertaining, attention grabbing ads. You're liable to win awards for best ads. But you also are liable to watch your competitors' sales figures out-race yours.

Does this mean that pictures aren't important? Although one university study demonstrated that verbal messages, without the presence of pictures, better persuade people to buy a product than verbal messages accompanied by pictures, many point out the benefits of pictures.[2] Great looking visuals can help hold interest. They can add entertainment. Like Tony the Tiger does for Frosted Flakes, they can reinforce what the core attribute of the product is. Visuals can help increase memory. *However, even though we might recall an ad because of a visual concept, we'll recall the product and its position because of a verbal concept.*

So no matter what you do, make sure your selling point can be expressed simply and verbally. That's how people remember your message. Rather than having a visual (computers and cows) at the very heart of your campaign, you must have a few short words (fights cavities) that succinctly describe who you are or what you do.

Advertising Power Secret #6: Make the heart of your message a verbal concept, not a visual one.

chapter 8

WRITING EFFECTIVE ADS

"I have discovered the most exciting, the most arduous literary form of all...I mean the advertisement...It is far easier to write ten passably effective Sonnets...than one effective advertisement."

Aldous Huxley, On the Margin (1923)[1]

A big killer of effective advertising campaigns is bad copywriting. Do all the right things to create demand, top-of-mind awareness and emotional attachment and still, your ad's message could ruin an otherwise stellar campaign.

You might recall the story of Joseph Pulitzer, who bought the *New York World* newspaper in the 1880s (and for whom the Pulitzer prizes are named). He once felt his newspaper was so powerful that it should be used to influence any creatures which might occupy other planets. So he proposed to put up an advertising sign in New Jersey that was so large, it presumably could be seen by anyone living on Mars. He scrapped the idea only when he was asked, "What language shall we print the sign in?"[2]

Pulitzer's sign, in and of itself, wasn't useless. It may have worked as a great vehicle for communication. But the *message* on the sign could foul everything up. The same concept is true if you were to pick up the telephone, call the local Mercedes[3] dealer, leave a message for him to have two free Mercedes in your driveway by the next morning, and then never hear back from him. Would you conclude that the telephone you used was useless? Absolutely not! Without a hitch, the phone would have allowed you to deliver your message, just as Pulitzer's sign would have. The problem again was the actual message. So too with advertising.

**Many designers of failed campaigns
blame the failure
on the advertising medium itself,
when all along the problem was the message.**

Great ads will make consumers comment on their desire for the product, not on how great the ad is. Effective advertisements focus on one point that sets your business apart from others. They motivate through emotions. They have headlines that sell. They're comprised of these and other essential elements. (For more details, see our special report, "Writing Advertising Copy That Sells").

Copywriting is a very critical element. Frequently getting your message to your prospects can do more harm than good if the essential elements of the message aren't in place.

Advertising Power Secret #7: Good copywriting has rules. Know them! Follow them.

chapter 9 | # COMMITMENT AND CONSISTENCY PAY

What can you expect from your ad campaigns? Through a continuing, consistent advertising program, you can create demand. You can gain top-of-mind awareness. Scores of people will think of your "brand" name first.

If this is your first foray into incorporating the correct frequency, copy, target and persuasive elements, plan on some start-up time before you begin seeing the fruit of your work. If consumers don't see you as a readily identifiable brand name then it will take the target group some time to get comfortable with you. Too many advertisers expect instantaneous results, but unless you're dealing with an *extremely* good limited time offer or sale, advertising's early results won't overwhelm you.

The real key is to be committed. You could have a very average marketing plan, but if you're committed to carrying it out, you'll get better results than someone with a brilliant plan and no commitment. This is not unlike investing. Traditionally, not much is gained by placing money into an investment fund for a short period of time, only to pull it out the first time the market wiggles. So too with advertising. You won't be able to show your accountant much of a return on your first couple of months of advertising. But like investing, you'll need to have the emotional constitution to stick with it through those start-up times. After all, you're building a long-term relationship with prospects.

Your advertising's initial impact will be on usage habits by people currently buying your product. At the same time, you'll get response from those who are currently in the market for what you sell. That response normally pales in comparison to what happens later. It's not uncommon during those initial months to feel like your advertising is a complete waste of money. By the sixth month, however, your ads should be paying for themselves. Correctly done, long-term ad campaigns more than pay for themselves. Short term ones usually don't. If you decide to advertise, be consistent. Hit your prospects over and over by advertising the same message in the same place.

> **The memorability and credibility building you need usually take at least three months to develop.**

It's often tempting to change your advertising message. Don't do it. All-State is still the good hands people. Crest still fights cavities. You can be flexible and change your ads, but don't change your message.

In all of this, know that you and all the people you associate with will get burned out on your ads and on your messages. The people who sold you advertising will grow weary of them. Their audiences will get tired of them. Ignore them. Don't change your ad until it quits bringing in money. If your ad sold homeowners' insurance to first-time home buyers last month, it likely will sell it to first-time home buyers next month.

Consistency and reinforcement are your real tickets to favorable results. Target an advertising vehicle you can afford and become the first brand name its audience thinks of.

Advertising Power Secret #8: Have a consistent message. Back it with commitment.

chapter 10 | **APPLYING THE EIGHT SECRETS OF POWERFUL ADVERTISING**

L et's review the eight key ingredients of a powerful advertising campaign.

1) Concentrate on frequency, not reach.
2) Use persuasion. Create demand.
3) Become memorable.
4) Target the right prospects.
5) Promote the right products.
6) Make the heart of your message a verbal concept, not a visual one.
7) Follow the rules for good copywriting.
8) Have a consistent message. Back it with commitment.

If you want to sell more of whatever it is you sell, these are the items you must address. On the converse, these are also the eight factors that, when misappropriated, can destroy an ad campaign. Mishandling any one of them can keep new customers from walking in the door.

The Media

Now that we know what needs to be accomplished, let's look at the media options before us. Certain advertising vehicles lend themselves naturally to most or all of these key components. Other venues only help us accomplish one or two critical elements.

Take reach and frequency as an example. We know that some advertising vehicles are more effective in reaching large groups of people. These typically would include newspapers, television, and direct mail. You'll recognize right away though, that the cost of advertising with these media often is so high that for most people, it's virtually impossible to use them enough to psychologically break through all the advertising clutter. That's where frequency options like radio and billboards normally come in. They're economical enough to allow you to buy enough ads to gain top of mind awareness with your potential customers. Following is more on the role each advertising option plays in fulfilling the eight keys to powerful advertising.

chapter 11 | NEWSPAPERS: THE INFORMATION MEDIUM

A small town newspaper once advertised, "Read your Bible to know what people ought to do. Read this paper to know what they actually do."[1]

Although newspaper circulation figures have been declining in recent years, the top metropolitan papers still reach large groups of people. And it reaches them with information. Information is what newspapers are all about and newspaper ads are no exception.

When a buyer wants information, this is the place to look. Newspapers are absolutely fantastic vehicles for reaching "right-now" buyers. Right-now buyers are people who have made a determination to buy a specific item that you happen to sell - right now.

"I've decided to buy a blue suit." (The decision has been made). "There are a couple of stores which I have confidence in and comfort with. Let's see which has the best deal or selection" (seeks information). The demand for the product is already in place. Now the consumer wants information. (Just the facts ma'am). She'll rifle through the newspaper to find out where to get a deal on a desired item.

You've likely done the same thing. When you've made the

emotional decision to buy, you look for and pay attention to specific newspaper ads - from all the listed features right through the price breakdowns. Newspapers are great at allowing you to provide detailed information, pricing and descriptions.

However, when a specific item isn't needed right this instant, the newspaper ads tend to get skipped. You can illustrate this principle on your own by answering a couple of questions. First, "How many newspaper ads do you remember from yesterday's paper?" If any, "Do you remember seeing any ads for pillows? If so, "From which stores?" Unless you've been looking for a special item, you probably don't remember any ads from yesterday's paper. (The memorable element is gone). And unless your pillow made your head feel like it rested on a brick all night long, you probably didn't take time to notice the pillow ads.

Newspapers will not draw new buyers into the market. They simply serve as an information medium reaching "right-now" buyers. Aside from this, newspapers also offer some small-scale ability to target. The TV section, sports section, classifieds and food sections all deliver different types of readers. And overall, newspapers do a splendid job at targeting older demographics.[2] In our fast-paced society, that's no surprise. With younger readers often taking just enough time to scan the front page (which has no advertisements) and a feature section, the older demographics are increasingly the ones perusing the entire paper. They, thus become more easily targeted through newspapers.

Newspapers also do an outstanding job in delivering reach. They'll potentially touch 50% of a metropolitan area.[3] Who wouldn't love to have all those people walking through the door? But unless you're a fairly large business, budget won't likely permit you to achieve any frequency with the newspaper. You'll be limited to reaching all of those people with a single exposure. With only one in nine ads "getting through," even putting an ad in the paper every day of the week still won't guarantee that you'll reach your intended customers enough times to effectively drive home your message. This lack of both frequency and the emotional impact of sound make it difficult to create top-of-mind awareness and product demand.

About the only way for the small division or business operator to achieve frequency in papers is to scale down from the daily morning paper to something much less widely read. There are usually plenty of smaller papers to choose from including neighborhood or community papers and shoppers. Depending on pricing, it can be possible to dominate these entities and therefore build frequency and consumer confidence.

Another way to attempt to gain frequency is to pick a page or a section, and on it, run consistently as large of an ad as you can afford. Then refer readers to your primary ad by running lots of tiny ads throughout the rest of the paper.

Overall though, the necessary component of frequency is best left to those media specifically designed for it. Frequency is not the name of the game here. Nor is creating demand or becoming memorable. Reach, plus information for right-now buyers are.

No doubt that with newspapers being so tangible (i.e. you can cut out your ad, put it in a folder and show it to anyone you wish), you psychologically will be tempted to build your whole campaign here. Don't. Regardless of your past success or lack thereof with newspaper advertising, you'll almost always do better when you lay a foundation for it with those media better built to create brand awareness and product demand.

The Newspaper Scorecard:

	Yes	No
Provides frequency & top-of-mind awareness?		✔
Creates emotional attachments and demand?		✔
Memorable?		✔
Efficiently targets specific groups of people?		✔
Allows you to make the right "offer"?	✔	
Can convey the central idea in words?	✔	
Provides for flexible copywriting?	✔	
Allows for a committed & consistent message?	✔	

chapter 12 | MAGAZINES: THE CONFIDENCE BUILDERS

Magazine advertisements go further towards building consumer trust and confidence than any other types of ads. Although that trust won't happen with just one ad, consistent contact with an ad over numerous issues can create a great deal of credibility. The process isn't immediate, so you need to have the budget to hang in there. (Some savvy business people try to speed the "frequency" process up by running ads in the classifieds section, following up the leads with a sales brochure and then a phone call). Regardless of the method, if you can build that confidence and trust, it'll turn into sales.

Like newspaper advertising, magazine advertising allows you to reach right-now buyers. If an individual is in the market for a particular item, and that purchase isn't contingent upon a time sensitive event (like a sale), that individual may also skim through magazines, looking for information on her desired purchase. And like newspapers, it's difficult to include critical power advertising elements like frequency and demand creation.

However, a key advantage of magazines is that people tend to take a lot of time to read them (unlike newspapers which are prone more to be skimmed for news). That includes time to read the ads. As such, long advertising copy can work extremely well. To the reader, reading a lengthy ad in a magazine is no different than reading a short article - which usually is why the magazine is being read in the first place. Take advantage of the amount of reading time that potentially will be dedicated to your ad.

Magazines also offer opportunities for very precise targeting. This is especially helpful if your product or service has its strongest appeal to a narrow niche of people. There's usually a magazine designed just for them. For example, if your product's appeal is to business owners, business magazines deliver your prospects. If your primary prospects represent an even smaller business niche, like bookstore owners or pet shop owners, often the best (or only) way to reach them is through industry trade magazines.

In summary, although magazines don't offer the powerful benefit of "sound," they do an effective job with targeting and with building consumer trust.

The Magazines Scorecard	Yes	No
Provides frequency & top-of-mind awareness?		✔
Creates emotional attachments and demand?		✔
Memorable?		✔
Efficiently targets specific groups of people?	✔	
Allows you to make the right "offer"?	✔	
Can convey the central idea in words?	✔	
Provides for flexible copywriting?	✔	
Allows for a committed & consistent message?	✔	

chapter 13 | DIRECT MAIL: IT'S ON TARGET

Direct mail is an option which can be very informative and can be extremely targeted. It's very easy to mail to people most likely to use your product or service. If your customers are young and single, you can mail to local apartment complexes. If your customers are in high income groups, you can mail to the higher income zip codes or neighborhoods. If your customers work at certain types of businesses, you can mail to those businesses. And if you're looking to develop repeat customers, direct mail allows you to communicate with all of your past clients.

A quality direct mail piece can also offer a longer "shelf life" than a newspaper ad. Some mailers can hang around a house for a few days. If the recipient reads your mailer and has interest in it, he or she likely will scan it a couple of times over a period of days, giving you the potential for several more impressions with that person.

But like other print media, this is not a venue which inherently delivers some of advertising's critical elements. You can't create top-of-mind awareness. Nor can you create product demand. And the best attempts at achieving frequent impressions encompass mailing a series of letters. If you can get them into the right hands and get them opened, you begin building some degree of familiarity and comfort. You'll have to weigh that against the norm of a 1-2% response rate and the fact that mailing lists become outdated quickly. Most estimates are that 15% or more of the people on a list move each year[1], and countless pieces are thrown away unopened.

The best way to prevent a quality, informative direct mail piece from flopping is to lay the foundation for that piece with an advertising vehicle that provides frequency. Otherwise, people see your piece once and then they throw it out. Or worse yet, they throw it out without opening it. And you fail to get inside of their minds often enough to make your business stand out.

The Direct Mail Scorecard:	Yes	No
Provides frequency & top-of-mind awareness?		✔
Creates emotional attachments and demand?		✔
Memorable?		✔
Efficiently targets specific groups of people?	✔	
Allows you to make the right "offer"?	✔	
Can convey the central idea in words?	✔	
Provides for flexible copywriting?	✔	
Allows for a committed & consistent message?	✔	

chapter 14 | YELLOW PAGES: "RIGHT-NOW" BUYERS

Y ellow Pages are the ultimate vehicle for reaching lots of people and the ultimate place for reaching "right-now" buyers.

Every home has the Yellow Pages. Almost 60% of all adults say they refer to the Yellow Pages at least once a week.[1] Yellow Pages reach the people who are ready to buy your product or service today. It's the only advertising option where, every time it's used, the user is serious about buying. In general, half of those who turn here will buy the product within 48 hours.[2] These people are choosing between you and all of your competitors who surround your ad. (Yellow Pages users look at nearly 5 ½ ads each time they open any given Yellow Pages section[3]).

To get noticed, you'll need to have as large a presence as your budget permits. Purchase decisions are being made here so give lots of reasons people should patronize your business. Really drill home your strongest benefit, and keep in mind that most users are simply looking for someone nearby. (Stressing your location or convenience can be vital).

As you're well aware, expensive as they may be, Yellow Pages in and of themselves do not make an advertising campaign. In reality, Yellow Pages are more of a directory than an advertising medium. Businesses that rely on Yellow Pages must wait for someone to come to them. Yellow Pages will not create additional demand or top-of-mind awareness. This medium's strength lies in its ability to reach and provide information to right-now buyers.

The Yellow Pages Scorecard	Yes	No
Provides frequency & top-of-mind awareness?		✔
Creates emotional attachments and demand?		✔
Memorable?		✔
Efficiently targets specific groups of people?		✔
Allows you to make the right "offer"?	✔	
Can convey the central idea in words?	✔	
Provides for flexible copywriting?		✔
Allows for a committed & consistent message?	✔	

chapter 15 | TELEVISION: THE BEST OF ALL WORLDS?

Television is able to cram more benefits into a single package than any other advertising alternative. People spend more time with television than with any other medium, and because it employs both sight and sound, it has the highest potential impact of all the advertising options. It's the first vehicle we've reviewed which is capable of creating an emotional attachment between consumers and products. This makes it capable of creating demand.

On top of delivering a persuasive, emotional impact, television also can reach very large groups of people. Although the 1990s have seen far fewer people citing TV as their primary entertainment form, the viewership levels are still quite high.[1] But like all media, the larger the audience, the more expensive it is to reach that audience frequently.

Without frequent deliveries of your message, your message will get overshadowed by others. That's a challenge which, in television, is compounded by commercial zapping. The average household changes the TV channel once every three minutes and 42 seconds. Those with cable flip channels once every three minutes.[2] And with the use of remote controls, it's not uncommon for a viewer to spend eight or so seconds per channel, while racing through 40 different channels. Commercials do get skipped.

Most major network affiliate stations sell most of their ads to bigger companies, represented by bigger advertising agencies. To get any sort of frequency out of television, it's not uncommon for agencies to purchase a schedule reaching 1½ times a particular demographic's population. If your city has 200,000 women ages 35 and older in it, and one ad reaches 1000 of them, an agency selling a product designed for these women would buy 300 ads. The 300 ads would deliver 300,000 advertising impressions to the target demographic (which is one and one-half times that target demographic's population). In real life, few have the budget to do this.

With major network-affiliated stations, the largest companies are about the only ones who can afford the frequency needed to create top-of-mind awareness. They do it through intensive, short-term schedules, or by airing the same TV ad for years and years (e.g. Life[3] cereal's "Give it to Mikey...he'll eat anything" commercials).

It does make sense to take a look at smaller stations in your market. The biggest audience size isn't important. Frequently reaching enough target customers to grow your business is. Like newspapers, it can make sense to downsize. Either go to a smaller station, or go to a section (in this case a program), which you can afford to dominate.

With the proliferation of cable and satellite channels, there is plenty of unsold (and affordable) commercial time available. Examine non-prime time programs, locally owned, independent stations and smaller cable outlets. Start looking for a beachhead there, a chance to capture a tiny bit of the market from which you can build.

Cable has become a popular option for many who cannot afford time on network affiliates. It allows you to target an audience somewhat better than network programming does. The major networks, as a whole, target huge masses of people across a wide demographic range. Individual programs narrow this down a little bit by each focusing on a particular demographic grouping.

On the other hand, cable often offers opportunity to target psychographically. As a general rule, a particular cable channel's viewers can be grouped and described by the attitudes, interests and opinions they share rather than by the ages, incomes or gender they have in common. You know that ESPN delivers sports lovers. You know that the History Channel delivers history buffs. If people with these attributes are important to your business, you know which cable channel delivers them, whereas it's more difficult to ascertain which programs they'll be viewing on traditional network TV.

Two of the main challenges for all TV advertisers are overcoming "zapping" and coming up with excellently produced commercials. Because of the zapping phenomena, some shrewd businesses have kept their logo in the corner of the screen throughout their commercial. They then fill the commercial with slickly produced images designed to entertain and hold the viewer's attention. The only downside is that in this process, many design the visuals purely for entertainment's sake. They forget to ensure that the visuals constantly reinforce the simple message of who or what the product is (see chapter 7, "The Power of Words").

When it comes to the production of commercials, it's not a bad idea to request that your ads not run next to national sponsors' ads. Production costs can get unwieldy as the average production cost on a thirty-second national ad in 1993 was nearly $180,000.[4] You won't spend that, but you won't want placed near the people who do either.

TV is often seen as a prestigious medium. Don't buy it because it gains you or your representatives prestige among peers. Instead, buy TV (network) to reach huge numbers of people. (And as with print advertising, lay a foundation for it with media that frequently break through the advertising clutter). Use TV's audio-visual one-two punch to emotionally impact the consumer's decision-making process and to create demand.

The Television Scorecard	Yes	No
Provides frequency & top-of-mind awareness?		✔
Creates emotional attachments and demand?	✔	
Memorable?	✔	
Efficiently targets specific groups of people?		
Network		✔
Cable	✔	
Allows you to make the right "offer"?	✔	
Can convey the central idea in words?	✔	
Provides for flexible copywriting?	✔	
Allows for a committed & consistent message?	✔	

chapter 16 | THE INTERNET: LOCATION, LOCATION, LOCATION

Location-wise, you hardly can beat showing up on your prospect's computer screen. The big question is, "Is it worth it?" Let's look at the big picture. First, dropping promotional dollars on the Internet comes in two general ways. Money can be used to build your own web site, providing information to current and prospective customers, or money can be used to advertise on others' web sites.

The first option actually extends what Yellow Pages advertising does. A Yellow Page ad and an Internet web site both reach right-now buyers. The Yellow Pages wait for right-now buyers to come and then provides them with a snippet of information. Similarly, a web page must wait for right-now buyers to arrive. But once they do, the page can provide reams of interactive information while working to turn visitors instantly into customers.

Advertising on another's web site carries the characteristics of magazine advertising one step further. Magazines are good at targeting distinct groups of people and providing them with information. The Internet allows you to narrow your target group even more. Rather than advertising in a magazine about computers, you narrow the target by going to a specific computer company's home page and advertising there. By doing this, you usually won't reach as many people as you would in other mass media, but virtually everyone you do reach is a qualified prospect.

Regardless of how you use the Internet, the Internet's greatest strength is its ability to provide instant feedback. People can immediately order your products, ask questions or be added to your mailing list. However, despite the excitement surrounding it, it generally does not deliver frequent exposures to your message. Even when you visit a given site often, it's not uncommon, while that site is loading, to scroll quickly through the page to the section or link you're interested in. Many will click on the link before the primary page fully loads, thereby missing the page's ads. Worse yet, some don't have their web browser's "image" option turned on, thus keeping many advertising images from showing up in the first place.

To combat this glaring challenge, several web site hosts have paid people with enhanced product offers or cash to read internet ads. And at least one internet service provider has promoted free monthly internet access (after an initial start-up fee) so long as users allow 30-second ads to follow them around the web. [1] So life is changing. Stay tuned.

The Internet Scorecard	Yes	No
Provides frequency & top-of-mind awareness?		✔
Creates emotional attachments and demand?		✔
Memorable?		✔
Efficiently targets specific groups of people?	✔	
Allows you to make the right "offer"?	✔	
Can convey the central idea in words?	✔	
Provides for flexible copywriting?	✔	
Allows for a committed & consistent message?	✔	

chapter 17 | BILLBOARDS: BUILDING FREQUENCY

W ant frequency? It's here! When you come upon a billboard, you can't somehow change the channel and miss it entirely. Because of that, billboards are able to generate, to the person who drives by regularly, the all-important three advertising impressions in a short time frame. And although you may come across four or five billboards in a row, it's generally easier to capture their messages than it is when you get one ad after another in Yellow Pages, newspaper, radio or TV.

Billboards' impact is limited only by the types of messages they can convey and by an inability to bring new buyers into the market (create demand). The best billboard messages will be informational, and will be short (no more than eight words). Short messages allow people who pass by to comprehend what it is you're trying to tell them. Short messages also allow you to print letters that are large enough to be read.

By default, short messages prevent you from providing all the necessary information to introduce new products or services. New products are better promoted through other media.

But short messages do allow you to quickly jog people's memories. In fact, billboards are most frequently used in a reminder role. Reminder advertising is appropriate in three situations. When current campaigns are running in other venues, reminder ads can reinforce and provide frequency for those ads. Reminder ads also can be used to support brand or product names which have been established for years and years (like milk or the YMCA). And such ads can remind you to make purchases that are seasonal.

Because of its reminder role, few companies can grow by using only billboard advertising. Billboards generally become the principle medium used only when the product or service can be used immediately by people driving by. Gas stations, motels and fast food restaurants often use this mode.

> **The two most powerful words in billboard advertising are "Next exit."**

You won't create demand, impact emotional decision-making or be memorable with billboards. But if you're after support for a widely recognized product, or if you're offering something that can be of quick use to those driving by, billboards can play an important role.

The Billboard Scorecard	Yes	No
Provides frequency & top-of-mind awareness?	✔	
Creates emotional attachments and demand?		✔
Memorable?		✔
Efficiently targets specific groups of people?		✔
Allows you to make the right "offer"?	✔	
Can convey the central idea in words?	✔	
Provides for flexible copywriting?		✔
Allows for a committed & consistent message?	✔	

chapter **18**

RADIO: THE POWER OF SOUND

Y ou'll recall from our earlier sections that "sound" plays an integral role in creating demand and in creating memorability. Couple that with the fact that between 6am and 6pm Americans spend more time with radio than with any other media[1], and radio becomes a very instrumental medium.

Radio is the only medium which allows you to incorporate each of advertising's eight power ingredients. Although radio stations don't reach as many people as newspapers and television do, and although they're not fit for describing detailed information, they are ideal for delivering a great deal of repetition.[2] Radio is one of just two advertising vehicles easily able to deliver frequency (the other is billboards) and, along with TV, is one of only two able to impact consumers *before* their decision to purchase has been made. *It can create demand.* Only after the latter occurs will people ever look for any information-oriented or price and item advertising that you do.

Radio also has an ability to deliver your message to any person, at any time at any place (home, work, car). Because it can break through the day's clutter and speak to people when comparatively-priced advertising venues cannot, it gets to people more frequently.

This intrusiveness further enables radio to improve the effectiveness of price and item or informational ads. For instance, radio can be used to specifically direct people to places where your information is. If you need space in the newspaper to list facts and details, first create demand and impact the decision-making process through broadcast media. Then use radio to direct people to the newspaper ad. If you've got a direct mail piece coming, radio can be used to prepare people for the mailing, and thus enhance your chances of having your mailer opened and responded to.

In essence, people see your written material and subconsciously say, "Oh yes, I've heard about this." You've come at them from more than one direction and started the process of building confidence and credibility through frequency, long before your mailer or print ad arrives in their home.

Having that frequency not only allows you to lay the framework for ads in passive media, it also allows you to speak to people throughout the entire buying process -

> **Frequency in radio is more readily affordable than in any other media.**

from the time they first hear of a product right up to the time they actually choose to buy it.

Additionally, many on-air personalities and even some stations in and of themselves have an intensely loyal following. They have enormous credibility. Getting these personalities behind you allows you to establish a very close and loyal relationship with consumers. You can develop extreme trust. Consumers who think the personality or station is credible, will likewise ascribe that credibility to the sponsors. This credibility factor is especially present among talk radio personalities, public stations (which, although they cannot accept commercials per se, do air sponsorship announcements) and stations reflecting the listeners' core lifestyle (like Christian stations). These stations' audiences are extremely prone to seek out and support sponsors "endorsed" by their favorite personality or station.

The Radio Scorecard	Yes	No
Provides frequency & top-of-mind awareness?	✔	
Creates emotional attachments and demand?	✔	
Memorable?	✔	
Efficiently targets specific groups of people?	✔	
Allows you to make the right "offer"?	✔	
Can convey the central idea in words?	✔	
Provides for flexible copywriting?	✔	
Allows for a committed & consistent message?	✔	

MEDIA RECAP

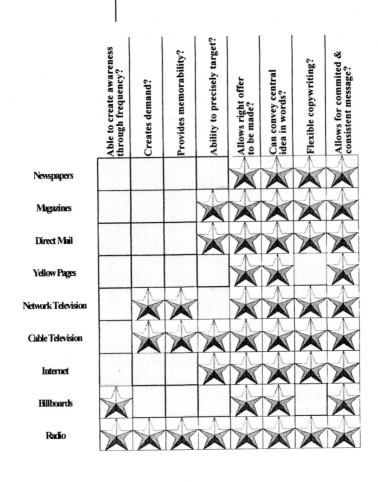

	Able to create awareness through frequency?	Creates demand?	Provides memorability?	Ability to precisely target?	Allows right offer to be made?	Can convey central idea in words?	Flexible copywriting?	Allows for commited & consistent message?
Newspapers					★	★	★	★
Magazines				★	★	★	★	★
Direct Mail				★	★	★	★	★
Yellow Pages					★	★		★
Network Television		★	★		★	★	★	★
Cable Television		★	★	★	★	★	★	★
Internet				★	★	★	★	★
Billboards	★				★			★
Radio	★	★	★	★	★	★	★	★

chapter 19 **SELLING MORE PRODUCTS: 10 RULES OF THUMB**

Certainly there are exceptions to the fundamental guidelines and principles this book presents. There are also times people win large sums of money in Las Vegas. It's just not very often. Here are ten rules of thumb to help you always experience the customer growth associated with powerful advertising.

1) All you want to do is sell product. Creativity alone does not do that. Keep your creativity within the confines of solid advertising principles, not in spite of them.

2) Worry about frequency before worrying about audience sizes. Even though it may cost the same, reaching a small group of people lots of times results in more sales than reaching huge numbers of people only once. Advertisements need to hit consumers three times before they can have any impact. To be sure your ad gets through at least three times, schedule it frequently.

3) Make your ads dominate a medium (or media entity). Run lots of ads in short time periods. This breaks through the advertising barrage, reaches your prospects and gains top-of-mind awareness.

4) Resist spending time and money to simply inform people.

Decisions to buy aren't made because of knowledge and information, but rather because of emotional factors.

5) For exceptional growth, concentrate on persuading people and creating demand for your product or service. Advertising vehicles employing sound provide the opportunities to do this by impacting the emotion-based decision-making process.

6) Enhance memorability by using media with sound. Being memorable helps retain top-of-mind awareness.

7) Know your target group.

8) Use a few short words to capsulize the essence of your message. Make sure the heart of your message is a verbal concept, not a visual one. Visuals help people remember seeing an ad. Concise verbal concepts help people remember the point of the ad.

9) Write good copy. Know the rules. Make it focus on a distinct position or emotion "owned" by your business. Failure to do so can ruin the best laid plans.

10) Become a long-term advertiser. Give your advertising campaign a chance to work. Confidence and credibility-building take a minimum of three months to build.

Free Reports
from **The Greater Business Institute**

The Greater Business Institute routinely provides informative business reports. Most are free, while others are available for a small fee. Get free reports instantly by calling our publisher's Fax-on-Demand system or by sending a self-addressed, stamped envelope to Franklin House Communications, P.O. Box 680035, Franklin, TN 37068-0035.

Free Business Reports Sent Instantly to Your Fax Machine
To get them, dial 1- 615-599-0137 and follow the prompts.
You must be calling from the handset of a fax machine.

---

110 - *Menu* of all available documents and reports. To keep up with the latest reports and publications from The Greater Business Institute, request this document frequently! 3 pages

112 - *Excerpt from the report "Tracking Advertising Results."* Enjoy this free preview! 2 pages.

113 - *Excerpt from the report "Writing Advertising Copy That Sells."* Enjoy this free preview! 3 pages.

115 - *Collecting Your Money* - Tips to make sure you actually collect what you've worked so hard to earn. 2 pages.

116 - *Why Advertise* - Eight positive effects your business receives from effective advertising campaigns. 1 page.

117 - *Glossary of Common Media Terms.* Is broken out by each of the major media categories, allowing you to get up to speed quickly with any advertising vehicle. 8 pages.

118 - *Why Customers Leave.* Learn the top reasons customers quit doing business with you. 2 pages.

119 - *Checking Potential Employee's References.* Before you hire any employee, ask references these 19 questions. Includes sample "permission to release information" statements. 2 pages.

SPECIAL REPORTS
(continued)

The following reports are available for a small fee. *Your satisfaction is guaranteed.* Individual purchasers may return any publication ordered directly from Franklin House Communications at any time, for any reason for a full refund. Act now and use the order form in the back of this book to order these tools today!

701 - *Writing Advertising Copy That Sells* is critical to your success. Your ad's copy is one element which can make or break any ad campaign. Institute the other seven elements of powerful ad campaigns and still, a bad ad could ruin your campaign. Bad ads can be humorous, entertaining and pleasing to the eye. You need to know how to identify them. Whether you're using print or broadcast media, this Report will show you the key principles to incorporate in every winning ad. *ISBN 0-9662692-0-9, 15 pages, digest size, $5.95 US dollars*

702 - *Tracking Advertising Results* shows you five key components of your marketing message to test, while providing the pros and cons of eight popular methods for measuring your advertising effectiveness. Without knowing how to measure advertising response, you're always in danger of scrapping a campaign that's about to make you rich. You'll learn the three types of profitable actions consumers make in response to your advertising. And you also will learn 10 different areas of your business which your advertising could impact. If you've ever felt your ads weren't pulling, or wondered how to accurately gauge response, this storehouse of information is for you. *ISBN 0-9662692-1-7, 10 pages, digest size, $4.95 US dollars*

---

* Rates guaranteed through 6/30/99. After this date, find current rates by calling our fax-on-demand system (1-615-599-0137).

appendix A | **NOTES & FOOTNOTES**

Preface-1 David Ogilvy, Confessions of an Advertising Man, 1963, chapter 3 as quoted by Tony Augarde, The Oxford Dictionary of Modern Quotations (Oxford, Oxford University Press, 1991); p. 136.

1-1 1982 speech quoted in Jay Conrad Levinson, Guerrilla Marketing - Secrets for Making Big Profits from Your Small Business (Boston, Houghton Mifflin Company, 1984); p. 155.

1-2 All brand and product names mentioned herein are trademarks or registered trademarks of their respective companies.

1-3 Radio Ink Magazine, March 17, 1997, p. 34.

1-4 Radio Ink Magazine, March 17, 1997, p. 35.

2-1 Michael J. Naples, Effective Frequency: The Relationship between Frequency and Advertising Awareness (New York; Association of National Advertisers, Inc., 1979), p. 67.

2-2 Herbert Krugman, "Why Three Exposures May Be Enough," Journal of Advertising Research, December, 1972 (New York; Advertising Research Foundation, 1972), pp. 11-14.

2-3 Kevin J. Clancy and Robert S. Shulman, Marketing Myths That Are Killing Business (New York; McGraw-Hill, 1994) pp. 163-164.

2-4 Thos. Smith, Hints to Intending Advertisers (London, 1885).

2-5 Radio Advertising Bureau "Sound Solutions" 1 par. Online <http://www.rab.com/station/whyradio//sound7.html> (3/8/97).

2-6 Jay Conrad Levinson and Seth Godin; Guerrilla Marketing Handbook (Boston; Houghton Mifflin, 1994), p. 34.

2-7 Cahner's Advertising Research Report "Is Brand Usage Driven by Advertising Exposure?" 1 par. Online <http://www.Variety.com:80/research/1305.htm> (8 Mar. 1997).

2-8 Naples, p. 72.
2-9 Naples, p. 73.
2-10 See brand and product trademark information in footnote 1-2.
2-11 Krugman, p 14.
2-12 For a related discussion, see Abbott Wool, "Frequency vs. Propinquity," Media Week, July 26, 1993; p. 19.

3-1 Radio Ink Magazine, January 29-February 11, 1996, p. 24.
3-2 A.H. Maslow, "A Theory of Human Motivation," Psychological Review, 50:370-386, 1943 as described in David L. Loudon & Albert J. Della Bitta, Consumer Behavior (New York, McGraw-Hill, Inc. 1979), p. 307.
3-3 Radio Ink Magazine, January 29-February 11, 1996, p. 21.
3-4 Jack Trout and Al Ries, Positioning (New York, McGraw-Hill in partnership with Warner Books, 1981), pp. 77-78.
3-5 See brand and product trademark information in footnote 1-2.
3-6 Tom Peters, Liberation Management (New York, Alfred A. Knopf, 1992), p. 660.

4-1 Dr. Elizabeth Loftus, University of Washington as quoted by the Radio Advertising Bureau, "Media Facts - Radio" 1 par. Online, <http://www.rab.com/station/mediafact/mfradio.html> (8 Mar. 1997).
4-2 See brand and product trademark information in footnote 1-2.
4-3 Larry C. White, Merchants of Death (New York, Beech Tree Books/William Morrow, 1988), p. 192.
4-4 People Weekly magazine 6/20/88 (New York; Time Inc., 1988); see back cover ad.

5-1 See brand and product trademark information in footnote 1-2.

6-1 See brand and product trademark information in footnote 1-2.

7-1 See brand and product trademark information in footnote 1-2.
7-2 Northwestern University study as cited by Jack Trout with Steve Rivkin, The New Positioning (New York, McGraw-Hill, 1996), p. 104.

8-1 Aldous Huxley, On the Margin, "Advertisement", (1923) as quoted by Robert Andrews, The Columbia Dictionary of Quotations (New York, Columbia University Press, 1993), p. 18.
8-2 Clifton Fadiman, The Little, Brown Book of Anecdotes (Boston; Little, Brown and Company, 1985), p. 458.

8-3 See brand and product trademark information in footnote 1-2.

11-1 E.C. McKenzie, 14,000 Quips & Quotes (Grand Rapids, MI, Baker Book House, 1980), p. 10.

11-2 While just over 50% of 18-34 year olds look at the paper daily, nearly 75% of those over age 55 do; Newspaper Advertising Association "Why Newspapers" 1 par. Online, http://www. naa.org/info/whynews/index.html> (3 Apr. 1997).

11-3 In 1995, over 60% of people over age 18 saw the daily newspaper; Newspaper Advertising Association "Why Newspapers" 1 par. Online, http://www.naa.org/info/Facts/facts1. html#MostUS> (3 Apr. 1997).

13-1 Lin Grensing, A Small Business Guide to Direct Mail (Bellingham, WA; Self-Counsel Press, 1991), p. 70.

14-1 Yellow Pages Publishers Association as quoted by the Radio Advertising Bureau, "Media Facts - Yellow Pages" 1 par. Online, <http://www.rab.com/station/mediafact/mfyellow.html> (8 Mar. 1997).

14-2 Barry Maher, Getting the Most from Your Yellow Pages Advertising (New York; AMACOM, a division of the American Management Association, 1988), p. 232.

14-3 See 14-1 above.

15-1 Jay Conrad Levinson, Guerrilla Advertising (Boston, New York, Houghton Mifflin Company, 1994), p. 245.

15-2 The Wall Street Journal, 4/25/88, p. 29.

15-3 See brand & product trademark information in footnote 1-2.

15-4 Jay Conrad Levinson, Guerrilla Marketing: Secrets for Making Big Profits from your Small Business (New York, Houghton Mifflin Company, 1993), p. 184.

16-1 As of 1/14/98, sites offering incentives to internet ad readers included http://www.cybergold.com & http://www.netcentives. com. On that date, the internet service provider referenced was http://www.freewwweb.com.

18-1 Media Targeting 2000 as quoted by the Radio Advertising Bureau website, "Media Facts - Radio" 1 par. Online, <http://www .rab.com/general/radinfo.html> (23 Feb. 1998)

18-2 Jack Z. Sissors and Lincoln Bumba, Advertising Media Planning (Lincolnwood, IL, NTC Business Books, 1993), p. 218.

appendix B | **INDEX**